British Columbia's Own Railroad

Lorraine Harris

hancock
house

ISBN 0-88839-125-0   Second Printing 1989

Copyright © 1982 Lorraine Harris

Cataloging in Publication Data

Harris, Lorraine, 1912-
British Columbia's own railroad

1. Pacific Great Eastern Railway (B.C.) —
History. 2. British Columbia Railway —
History. I. Title.
HE2810.P2H37   385'.065'711   C82-091224-7

Editor Rihji Manopi
Typeset by Lisa Smedman in Times Roman on an AM
  Varityper Comp/Edit
Production & Cover Design Crystal Ryan
Layout Laura Moffat
Photos A.L. Grinke
Illustrations Crystal Ryan
Printed in Hong Kong

Hancock House Publishers Ltd.
19313 Zero Avenue, Surrey, B.C., Canada V3S 5J9

Hancock House Publishers
1431 Harrison Avenue, Blaine, WA 98230

Table of Contents

To Linda and Bob

Beginnings

For many years, and even today, isolated communities throughout British Columbia have depended upon the railroad for their very survival. This vital link was pushed through some of the most difficult and rugged terrain in Canada by the Pacific Great Eastern (PGE) and its parent companies. This tradition of linking the hinterland with the rest of British Columbia is carried on today by the modern British Columbia Railway (BCR). But train enthusiasts can still recapture the experience of traveling by steam locomotive on the Royal Hudson, which travels from North Vancouver to Squamish. The BCR is a working railroad,

Newport Beach, Squamish, B.C., 1913.   BCR Audio Visual Services

hauling freight and passengers from North Vancouver to Fort Nelson and Driftwood, and maintaining contact with other places not connected by road.

The PGE, now the BCR, has facetiously been known as "Neither Pacific, Great, nor Eastern," "Past God's Endurance," "Please Go Easy," and "Prince George Eventually." The first official name of the railroad was the Howe Sound, Pemberton Valley and Northern Railroad. This company was formed April 25, 1907 with the idea of using the railroad to help logging operations. The first phase was to have track laid from Newport Beach, now Squamish, to D'Arcy at the west end of Anderson Lake. Sixty- to seventy-pound rails (weight per yard) were laid, and the tracks followed the Squamish and Cheakamus rivers and the old Pemberton Trail. A ten-ton 0-4-0 tank locomotive of English construction was used on this track.

First Tracks

The Howe Sound, Pemberton Valley and Northern became the Howe Sound and Northern in 1910, and was renamed the Pacific Great Eastern on February 12, 1912. Sixty years later it became the British Columbia Railway and is said to cover one of the most scenic routes of any railroad.

"Pacific Great Eastern" has had many connotations for many people, but few know the origin of the name of this important railway. The railroad, then called the Howe Sound and Northern, had, as financial backers, the Great Eastern Railroad of England. It was to honor this company that the Howe Sound and Northern

Rail dock, Squamish, B.C., 1914.

The first engine used by the HS&N (Howe Sound and Northern) Railway, Squamish, B.C.

BCR Audio Visual Services

BCR Audio Visual Services

8

A log dump in operation during the 1930s, Squamish, B.C.

owners adopted the Pacific Great Eastern name. Other names had been proposed: The "Ashcroft, Barkerville, Fort George," the "Naas and Skeena Rivers Railway," the "Peace and Naas Railway," the "Vancouver and Coast Kootenay," and the "Kootenay and Athabaska."

In the early days track was laid 2,600 ties to the mile, and pit-run ballast (rock straight from the pit) was used. Today, track is laid 3,200 ties to the mile, and crushed rock is used for ballast, making it safer and easier to level the roadbed.

In 1910 the Grand Trunk Pacific Company surveyed a route up the Fraser River, Harrison River, and Harrison Lake to Lillooet and Prince George. This route was found to be too difficult and costly, and the Grand Trunk Pacific abandoned the idea. This survey later became a part of the PGE track bed.

In 1911 the Howe Sound and Northern ran a survey from Lillooet to Squamish for a possible rail route. This survey was made on the west side of the Cheakamus River, and the rails were

Laying track in the early days.

laid from Squamish to Cheekeye. The railroad hauled logs from Cheekeye to saltwater at Squamish for the W.H. Day Lumber Company of Vancouver.

The PGE was originally incorporated under Provincial Charter on February 27, 1912, to construct and operate a railway along Howe Sound from Vancouver to Newport Beach and on to Lillooet. From here, it was to travel east 470 miles to Fort George, where it would join with the Grand Trunk Pacific. Foley, Welch and Stewart, a railroad construction company, was given the contract. Construction commenced at both the southern end (North Vancouver) and north of Squamish to Cheekeye. They surveyed the east side of the Cheakamus River and decided that this was a better route than the previously surveyed west side. They graded and built the railroad on the east side and went ahead quickly, considering the difficult terrain they had to contend with. The rock faces and chasms presented problems, but rails were laid to Alta Lake in 1914 and to Lillooet in 1915.

While the railway was being built from Squamish, north; in North Vancouver, track was being laid west. North Vancouver was later to become the southern terminus of the PGE. In July 1913 the thirteen miles of track from North Vancouver to Whytecliffe was started, using the same size rail as that used at Newport Beach, and, in January 1914, the service between Lonsdale, North Vancouver, and Dundarave in West Vancouver was inaugurated. Two gas cars were put into use. These were the first of the Halls and Scott cars, #101 and #102, to be put into operation. There were several stops, and these were a great convenience to North Shore residents, as transportation was at a minimum and the North Vancouver ferry was the only Burrard Inlet transportation. Leaving North Vancouver, the stops were: Capilano, 14th Street, Hollyburn, Weston, and Dundarave. By April 4, of the same year, service extended to Whytecliffe.

In 1915 freight was barged to Squamish from North Vancouver, and passengers went via Union Steamship to Squamish. The Terminal Navigation Company, which provided this service, was owned by the well-known Cates family of North Vancouver.

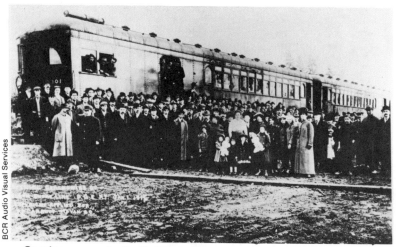

Opening ceremonies for the North Shore line of the PGE, North Vancouver, January 1, 1914.

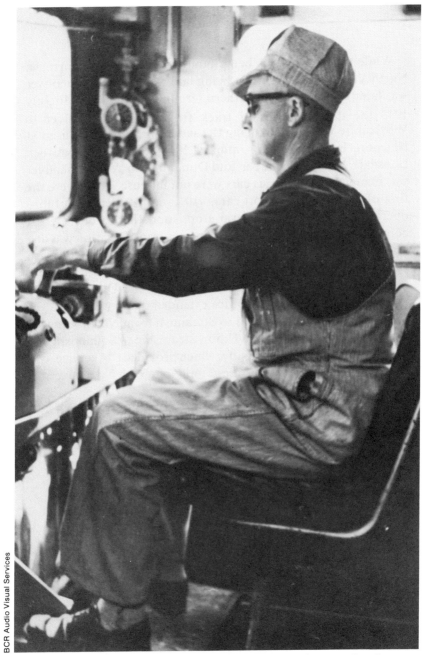

Experienced engineers came great distances to operate the new railroad.

In 1918 all construction was stopped by the outbreak of World War I. At this time, the Foley, Welch and Stewart Company gave up as contractors of the railroad, and the British Columbia government acquired the capital stock and made plans to extend the line. The renewed construction of this railroad attracted men from all over the continent. Older railway men came to help operate the new wilderness railroad, and their experience helped surmount many problems. As the older men retired, younger men took their places and continued to build and operate the railroad. This line was important to an area that had been without transportation (other than packtrain) since 1860, when the Royal Engineers built the road from Port Douglas to Lillooet. In the early days of tough grades and roadbeds blasted out of rock cliffs, engineers not only had to operate their engines but had to be mechanics, inventors, as well as offer prayers on many occasions.

Mt. Garabalda, PGE Railway, 1913.

The Phillipses of Rainbow Lodge

Before the railroad was built, a young Vancouver couple, Alex and Myrtle Phillips, had established their fishing lodge at Alta Lake. They walked into Alta Lake in 1911 and 1912 to fish the plentiful trout and found themselves enamored of the country. Consequently, they bought 100 acres of wilderness and lakeshore to start a lodge, which they named Rainbow Lodge after the magnificent rainbows they had seen there. As the railroad construction crews neared Rainbow Lodge, the men were more than happy to be able to enjoy Myrtle Phillips's good cooking. They had construction camps at regular intervals, but their own

Railroad stop, Alta Lake, B.C.

PGE passengers relax by the fire after a dinner at Rainbow Lodge.

cooking and housekeeping held no great attraction. As the rails were laid to Rainbow Lodge and on to Mons Wye, near Green Lake, the engineer of the work train—often as early as 5:30 a.m.—would give a single howling blast of his whistle about a mile before the lodge, and Mrs. Phillips would get up and greet him when he stopped there. He would call out, "When can you feed the crew?" She would reply, "Give me half an hour," and when the train returned from Mons Wye (a wye was a track used for turning a steam engine that couldn't back up) half an hour later, she would have a delicious breakfast of porridge, bacon and eggs, toast, and lots of steaming coffee ready for them. For this

Rainbow Lodge with its own store and post office, Alta Lake, B.C.

17

Rainbow Cottage, Alta Lake, B.C.

she collected meal tickets from each crew member, which were later redeemed by the PGE for thirty-five cents each. This was a small price, but it was necessary for this hard-working couple's very existence until the passenger trains came through in 1915, bringing guests for the lodge and passengers to feed.

On the early trains the passenger cars were hitched on behind the freights, and there were no dining cars. Mrs. Phillips was informed by phone from Squamish how many passengers desired lunch, and the train would stop at Rainbow Lodge long enough for them to eat. On the way south she would be informed how many wanted dinner, and again the train stopped long enough for them to be served. It was not an easy task for a young city woman to serve hot, fresh food, as the trains were rarely on time and Rainbow Lodge had only a wood stove. Yet somehow she managed, and she was always praised for her excellent meals. Myrtle Phillips said the friends they made amongst passengers and crew made all the difficulties worthwhile.

Later, another stop that catered to passengers and crews was D'Arcy, where a summer lodge was built. The owner, a very religious man, charged fifty cents a meal and often gave a free lecture to crew members who used coarse language.

Snowbound

The railway was faced with inclement weather each winter, and the snowfall was often enough to hamper its schedule, at times forcing trains to a standstill. In 1916 a snowplough and train were forced to a stop about one mile south of Pemberton in MacDonald's Cut, where there was twenty feet of snow. Because the railway was the only way out, the trainmen were stranded. The train crew managed to walk the mile to Pemberton, but it took them almost two hours to struggle through the deep snow. The snowplough crew came up later and stayed at the Pemberton Hotel. As there were no freights moving, it was not long before

Engine No. 578 snowbound in MacDonald's Cut near Pemberton, B.C.

BCR Audio Visual Services

A passenger examines the track as the snow continues to fall.

the extra "guests" taxed the stores at the hotel. The townspeople too were feeling the pinch of the lack of supplies.

These railway men, who were enterprising fellows and hardy types in a tough business, decided it was time to get out of Pemberton; and those who didn't have or couldn't get snow-shoes, made skis from split cedar and laced them on with buckskin thongs purchased from the Indians. When all were shod for snow travel, they left Pemberton and headed out for Squamish. They finally arrived at Rainbow Lodge, where they stayed overnight and enjoyed warm beds and good meals. When they left the next day, it was eight degrees below zero Fahrenheit. Fred Clutterbuck, an older man, remained at the lodge for three days to rest up after the first part of the trek. Supplies at Rainbow were running low. Mrs. Phillips decided to go out with the railroaders, as she had planned to travel to the coast anyway. She donned skis and kept up with the men all the way. It was so cold that the eggs which they had purchased from settlers during the trip froze solid. They traveled to Brandywine, twenty-eight miles from Squamish, and, to their delight, an engine had bucked the weather to come to meet them.

Disasters

The men of the PGE had many hair-raising experiences. There were numerous tragedies during the early days of the railroad: deaths, near-deaths, fires, floods, and derailments. One of the worst tie-ups was in 1922, when one and a half miles of track were washed out by heavy rains north of Daisy Lake and no trains went through for seven weeks.

The engineers of the old steam locomotives felt that with a little ingenuity and a package of rolled oats for plugging any holes in the boiler tubes (the oatmeal swelled in the boiling water and plugged the rust holes), they would always be able to limp their faithful engines home. Unlike the present-day diesels, the steam engines were able to shift all their power onto one side if necessary. Should the problem be going over rocks on one side of the roadbed, the steam could be cut from the disabled side and the engine could run on the other side.

BCR Audio Visual Services

Railroad camps, consisting of makeshift tents, provided shelter for the track crews.

There have been many slides along the PGE route, since it was blasted out of sheer rock faces and there was a great deal of shattering in the rock formation. Each winter as the temperature dropped, the frost penetrated the fissures and, come spring and the thaw, the rock pieces let go, resulting in a slide. Each summer, track crews investigated these areas and searched for rock that looked like it might let go. Using explosives, they brought it down to avoid as many slides as possible. The dirt or mud slides, usually caused by heavy rains, were sometimes as difficult to clear as rock slides. In the summer the track crew included a crewman who traveled the track in a flatcar to examine the trackbed to make sure there were no fires. Fire was a hazard for the crews; when the train braked, the friction between track and wheels caused sparks to fly.

The North Shore suffered a very bad railway accident in 1917 when a gas car, #103, contained in the second section of a split train leaving North Vancouver, collided with a steam train that had been on the Whytecliffe siding when the first section passed.

A landslide disables a PGE line.

Unaware that it was a two-section train, the steam train pulled out traveling east, meeting the 103 head-on, just east of the train trestle that used to cross Marine Drive at Travers, slicing the 103's motor down the middle. It was a miracle no one was killed, although a great number were injured. This was the first of the gas cars "to leave the service."

There have been countless accidents involving the railroad, a number of them caused by slides. As reported in the railroad magazine *The Steam Chest*, one such slide occurred "on the evening of August 12, 1944, when locomotive #156 was knocked off her tracks by a slide caused by a cloudburst loosening rocks in its wake, at old mile-95 (from Squamish) taking her crew to their glory." She was hit by the slide and thrown in to Anderson Lake, landing on a ledge just under the water-line, but the currents took her off the ledge and to the bottom of the lake before salvage operations could be started. Since she was the engine on a passenger train, it is a great wonder that more lives were not lost. Fortunately, the passenger cars somehow remained topside.

Six years later, in January of 1950, engine #153 was pushed into Seton Lake by a snowslide only a few miles from where #156 went into Anderson Lake. The crew and engine went to a watery grave. The sides of these two lakes are practically devoid of lakeshore, with the precipitous mountains rising up from the lakeside, making salvage almost impossible.

A blow up caused another accident but, fortunately, no loss of life. On September 23, 1951, a novice engine watchman at the Quesnel roundhouse let a fire burn in the firebox and then left the engine. Returning later, he found no water showing in the glass and turned on the injector, a fatal mistake for engine #161. Hot steel and cold water do not mix, and #161's crown sheet let go in a massive explosion. After the debris had stopped falling, it was found that the watchman, though blown through the tender, was miraculously alive and uninjured. But #161 had literally disintegrated. The training truck was blown into the ground, the frame was snapped, and the drivers showed signs of being driven off the axles. Over a quarter of a million horsepower had been unleashed by the hot water turning to steam. The watchman was seen again, just long enough to be fired.

A train wreck after a firebox explosion in Quesnel, B.C. BCR Audio Visual Services

The locomotives on this railroad were faithful old steam engines until 1947, when two diesels, a ninety-ton General Electric and a sixty-five-ton General Electric center cab switcher, were brought in. A gas electric engine had been tried, but it had proven unsuccessful.

Delays were numerous and frequent, for many reasons. Slides, track trouble, burned bridges, and forest fires all affected the timetable. The PGE was not noted for being on time; however, on one occasion the train arrived at the station and the conductor was congratulated for being punctual. He was in the difficult position of explaining that this was yesterday's train—twenty-four hours late. Sometimes the delays gave the crew some slack time, and the crew were seldom without fishing poles in their quarters. Many a feed of stream or lake trout was the reward for an aggravating delay.

B.C. Travel Bureau

A Rubber Neck open observation car, Anderson Lake, B.C.

Tracks are laid across an expanse of lumber to complete this typical railway bridge.

Crewmen were seldom at a loss for action. One incident that could have caused consternation and delay was averted by this kind of speedy reaction. The incident occurred when a brakeman was left at Birken. This could have been a real problem, as the brakeman does the switching for trains moving to and from sidings. However, he handled the situation in a very practical manner by hopping a speeder (a small motorized railcar) and catching up with the train at D'Arcy.

In the past the PGE had been a carefree railroad. If a passenger missed his stop, the train just backed up and let him off. If a hunter shot some game, the train stopped until he brought his prize to the baggage car. Guns were carried in the baggage cars then, as is still the practice, for killing animals hit by the train.

Engineer Angus McCrae saved a train, crew, and passengers on one occasion by means one could only describe as psychic. As his train approached Cheakamus Canyon, he had a strange feeling and, almost involuntarily, stopped the train before the bridge. The conductor rushed forward, and when he asked McCrae why he had stopped the train, McCrae replied, "I don't know. I just stopped it. Let's look at the bridge." Nothing looked amiss on the topside of the bridge, but upon investigating they found that a huge rock had come down the steep canyon sides. Although it hadn't touched the top of the bridge, the underpinnings were knocked loose and hung swaying. But for McCrae's sixth sense, both train and bridge would have crashed into the river.

Looking Out the Window

On September 14, 1914, construction of fifty-eight miles of track from Cheekeye past Pemberton began. By 1915 the work and passenger trains were stopping at the Lillooet station. The station was below Lillooet and on the north side of Cayoosh Creek at the confluence of the Fraser, where a huge wooden railroad bridge was built across the river. It was not until 1931 that the station was moved to downtown Lillooet. By December 1915 the railroad extended to Chasm north of Clinton, and it was extended on to Quesnel and Prince George in 1917 and 1918, respectively. The construction of the track up the east side of the

Crossing the river at Lillooet.

Near Fountain, B.C.

Seton Lake, east of Lillooet. →
A.L. Grinke

The first PGE logo as it
appeared in 1914.

The BCR near Clinton.

A.L. Grinke

Stone Creek Bridge. A.L. Grinke

The BCR follows the curve at Pavillion.   A.L. Grinke

The PGE logo as it
appeared in 1959.

Construction of a 10.2 mile bridge in West Vancouver.   A.L. Grinke

The Quesnel River Bridge.

Seton Lake near Lillooet.

A.L. Grinke

The Royal Hudson leaving one of the many tunnels on the trip from North Vancouver to Squamish, B.C.

The spectacular Chieftan Mountain stands behind the Royal Hudson as it leaves Squamish, B.C.

A.L. Grinke

Lillooet Bridge.

Replacing track above the Fraser River.   B.C.R. Audio Visual Services

The BCR logo as it appears today.

Glen Fraser.

A freight train near Fountain, B.C.

Fraser from Lillooet was another major feat. The grade was steep, the terrain unsettled, and in many spots the track was practically hanging out over steep canyons as the train approached the village of Fountain.

In this area the land is terraced, and it was used occasionally for growing hay. The track would then step up another grade to another plateau and into the beautiful scenery of mountains and meadows, in the area known as Pavillion. From here the train goes around Pavillion Mountain and down a steep grade to Pear Lake, which was named by the Royal Engineers for its pear shape. The line then continues on to Clinton. From there on, the railroad is in Cariboo country and the scenery, although changed, is equally interesting. Natural meadows, pine trees, and grazing cattle appear against a backdrop of mountains in the distance. The track rejoins the Fraser River Valley north of Williams Lake, and the river contributes to the wildness of the scenery.

A European gentleman making the trip on the old observation car, during the 1940s was heard to say, "I have traveled very extensively in the European Alps but never have I seen scenery to equal or outdo this dramatic scenery."

It was in those "good old days" that the train trip offered dining car service, sleeping cars, and an observation car with seats facing the windows for a full view of the spectacular scenery. In contrast to the mountains of Cheakamus Canyon, there were the placid waters of Anderson and Seton Lakes. Their mirrorlike surfaces reflected the neighboring mountains, except when the "devil winds," as the Indians called them, whipped the waters to a froth.

Three engines pull a freight train, Interior, B.C.

Crossing the Cheakamus Canyon Bridge.

Lillooet is the entrance to the beauties of the Fraser River. Near Lillooet, the railroad passes the local Indian fishing grounds where they used to wield their large nets from the rock bluffs. Upstream from here the railroad bridge still takes the PGE-BCR to the steep banks of the east side of the Fraser. The train winds its way along the canyon, making one feel as if he were riding in a sky-tram with the river flowing and twisting far below. After rounding the well-known Pavillion mountain, the track drops down swiftly into the valley on the way to Clinton. From here the ranches and rangeland remind one of the tales of the pioneers who built this country.

Special Deliveries

When the PGE Company realized that the route from Whytecliffe to Squamish was impossible in 1915, freight was barged from Vancouver to Squamish by the Terminal Navigation Company, and passengers went on the Union Steamship on a circuitous route of Howe Sound to connect with the PGE, arriving there to meet the train's scheduled departure at 1:30 p.m. The Union Steamship captains got very frustrated when their sailing time was delayed because the freight cargo of liquor for the interior had to be checked. The liquor would arrive at the dock in Vancouver in horse-drawn drays; then it had to be

Log hauling near Squamish, B.C.

counted as it was loaded and recounted at Squamish. It is a good thing time was not so much of the essence in those days, as schedules were often disrupted by circumstances like this. The barge service continued until 1957, and then all freight was hauled out of the North Vancouver terminal. By then it was situated at the foot of Pemberton Avenue, a short distance from the original depot.

Alcohol for the interior presented problems at the coast, but there was one time when the same type of cargo presented problems in the interior. It was in 1920 at McCalister, then the end of the rail line. Prohibition was enforced in British Columbia, and liquor—both name and article—was taboo. As a result, all freight on trains was scrutinized. Word got out that forty-one cases of liquor were coming to McCalister. As it turned out, it was farther north.

The manager of the railroad aboard the Union Steamship en route to Squamish noticed the cargo and became suspicious. A short time later he ran into a police sergeant on the boat and reported his suspicions. The cargo was assigned to McCalister, and the manager said he'd like to continue along with it and examine it there. The policeman agreed to follow the work train to see what was going on.

At McCalister there were only three families: the Sidsworths, who were with the PGE; a rancher; and a postmaster. Apparently Spike Sidsworth was something of a character, for when he was asked by the police for which stop the cargo was destined and for what, he replied he'd had an order to hold it, "and that's what I'll do." The sergeant had to go back to his post in Williams Lake. However, having been told of the situation, he had to find out who owned the liquor. He decided to stay overnight to see if it would be picked up. This presented a real problem, as there was no accommodation. When he asked Spike where he was going to sleep, it turned out the Sidsworths had no room and Spike said, "The postmaster's place is alive with kids, and the rancher's place is alive with vermin." So the sergeant went back to Williams Lake saying he would come back to check on the freight. He did, and Sidsworth told him it was unclaimed and still in the barn covered with hay. Because the police were more interested in who was responsible than in the dispostion of the liquor, he left again, admonishing Spike to notify him if it was claimed.

Loading cattle, Williams Lake, B.C.

A cattle drive to Williams Lake, B.C.

A few days later Sidsworth received a message saying the shipment would be picked up. A truck arrived at midnight, and the driver loaded the cases by lanternlight. Then he gave Spike the delivery sheet and went weaving on his way. Apparently needing some sustenance, the driver sampled the cargo and later began depositing the cases in barns along the way. A farmer named Livingston, on going out to feed the animals, came upon two cases in the barn, one empty and one full. He went in to tell his wife of the find, and when they went to look it was gone. It was assumed that the driver revived enough to remember what he had done and came back to pick the case up.

40

The cargo finally got to the Chinese in the Quesnel area, who apparently were distributing it in pig-swill barrels.

Spike was in trouble with the police sergeant for not having informed him of the removal of the shipment. His excuse was, "It was too late to call."

And then there was the time, in later years, when a refrigerator car left the Pemberton station in North Vancouver, went up the line, and was returned to the North Vancouver yard. The next day someone noticed the car still had the lock on and opened it to find that a whole carload of beer had made the return trip and never found its destination. There must have been some thirsty people up the line.

Place Names

In the past mail was delivered to isolated spots from the freight car of the PGE. A mail sack was dropped if no freight necessitated a stop. The people along this route—farmers, ranchers, and trappers—were once more brought in touch with the coast and could "shop" from their own homes.

In the early days the PGE served the people of its territory; it delivered mail and freight, and even greeted settlers who lived far from the Cariboo road and picked up their produce for market. The long list of stops from North Vancouver to Prince George indicates the service given. Today the stops are essentially centers

Brandywine Falls cascade into Daisy Lake.

that are a nucleus for a few villages along the route.

The train stops have interesting names, and the stops from Prince George north were all named by one man, Roy Drage, who was traffic manager when the north line was opened. Many of these stops were named for the people who lived there—homesteaders, ranchers, and farmers. Other stops have Indian names, some are named for the terrain, and a few are in memory of well known World War I events. In addition a number are named for interesting reasons. One such name is Brandywine. Two surveyors working in the area were standing at the bottom of the nearby falls that cascade down a great height into Daisy Lake. They disagreed on the height of the falls, and a bet took place. One said, "I have a bottle of brandy that says I'm right." Not to be outdone, the other said, "Well, I've got a bottle of wine that says I'm right." They proved who was right, named the falls Brandywine to commemorate the event, and then proceeded to consume both bottles on the spot.

There are several other stops with interesting origins to their names. Squamish is an Indian name meaning, "Mother of the winds." Lillooet is another Indian name. Apparently it is a name of many meanings, one of which is "the meeting of three waters"—Cayoosh Creek, Bridge River, and the Fraser. It was also a boom town from 1858 to 1860, when miners rushed to the goldfields at Barkerville.

Distances from Lillooet on the Cariboo Road were applied as names to wagon stops. 70- and 100-mile houses later became towns of the same name. Other names were more imaginative. It is believed when Whiskey Creek was named it was just automatic that Soda Creek must follow. AngusMac was the combination of a man's name, while Chetwynd was named for a minister of the province.

45

When the train used to arrive at Clinton (around 6:00 to 6:30 a.m.) passengers wishing accommodation at the hotel found a note on the door, "Room #1 open. Please do not disturb." And when one was awaiting the arrival of the southbound train, the train's whistle could be heard for miles on a clear night. To the uninitiated, this could mean several trips to the platform with baggage in hand to stand beside the signal lanterns, only to hear the sound fade into the dark. The frustrated passenger would have to plod back to the station, which was often just a shed, to await the next blast and repeat the procedure. By the time the train arrived, the passenger was often an exhausted disbeliever, only too glad to finally climb aboard. And if he was lucky enough to find a berth, he would be rocked to sleep by a seemingly angry hand rocking the train. The roadbed left much to be desired for smooth travel, particularly around the many turns.

Finishing Touches

The officers of the PGE were important to its progress, and some fought long and hard for its very existence. Others just didn't know what to do with it, as, at times, it was a great financial problem.

The first chairman was D'Arcy Tate, elected April 4, 1912, and the first president, J.S. Stewart, was elected a year later. The past and present officers of the PGE-BCR make a long and distinguished list of names, and to these men we owe a debt of gratitude for building this lifeline to British Columbia's interior.

The political aspects of the railroad were often far-reaching

The Inaugural train. Among those pictured are W.A.C. Bennett, Einar Gunderson, P.A. Gaglardi, and R. Williamson.

The PGE bridge in Quesnel provides picturesque scenery for picnickers.

and confusing, but her financial ups and down were something else again. In 1942 Premier "Duff" Patullo offered the PGE to the Federal Government. According to Patullo, "We nominally owe Ottawa $35 million in treasury bills against which we claim $25 million as chargeable to employment relief and property— the obligation of the Dominion Government. I suggest the Dominion Government wipe out the $25 million item and we turn the PGE over to them free of all charges." This was a political gem that passed by quietly. Then in 1945 Premier John Hart offered the PGE to the Canadian National and the Canadian Pacific Railroads, but neither wanted it. The threat of sale to U.S. interests during World War II when the United States

BCR Audio Visual Services

50

sought a connection from the contiguous states to Alaska, as the Japanese were posing a real threat to the Aleutians. Premier John Hart then changed his mind, saying, "The PGE deserves a better fate than to be sold off, even for a lot of dollars." A second threat of American takeover happened in 1947, but this too, was turned down.

The northern routes were completed to Quesnel in 1921, and this was the northern terminus until 1952. The last spike on the Quesnel-Prince George connection was driven at Ahbou Creek Bridge November 1, 1952, and a ceremonial train went north for

W.A.C. Bennett and Miss Peace River open the Fort St. John line.

Driving the last spike, Dawson Creek Inaugural Run.

Loading lumber in the interior of B.C.   BCR Audio Visual Services

this event. In 1956, construction commenced on the line from Prince George to Dawson Creek and Fort St. John, but it was 1958 before the first train crossed the Peace River. July 7, 1958, saw the first commercial freight services into Fort St. John. On October 2, 1958, the "last spike" connecting the Dawson Creek line was driven, and a day later the same ceremony was repeated on the Fort St. John branch. Three special trains ran from North Vancouver to Fort St. John for this occasion. A spur line was built in 1966 from Kennedy, 100 miles north of Prince George, to the instant town of McKenzie to further the development of the rich resources of the north country. Fort St. James was connected on October 18, 1967, but the official opening took place in August of 1968. Extensions were built from Odell to Tajla Lake, eighty miles northwest of Fort St. James, to service this rich timber region, and from Fort St. James to Nelson, a distance of 250 miles, to "link the north by rail with all the markets of the world."

Gefferson Lake petro-
chemicals bound for Port
Mellon, August 2, 1958.

Einar Gunderson inside
PGE Engine 581.

53

Another feature of good planning for future development was the realization of the sprawling PGE Industrial Park at Prince George, which comprised 1,382 acres to be developed for both heavy and light industry. The PGE prepared for the light industry by clearing and partially grading the area and by installing roads, water facilities, and tracks. For heavy industry the PGE provided roads, and companies had to install their own services. The rail line extensions together with the new industrial park made possible the utilization of previously inaccessible forest regions. This construction, combined with the advent of the northern power project and development of surrounding forest and agricultural areas, attracted money for building. It also opened up the grain elevators at Groundbirch, Dawson Creek, and Taylor, and the pulp mills at Prince George and Quesnel, to say nothing of numerous sawmills.

It wasn't until 1956 that the railroad was completed from Horseshoe Bay to Britannia. The operation used over two million pounds of dynamite and had to create four tunnels to make a roadbed along Howe Sound's rugged shoreline. Track had previously been laid to connect Britannia to Squamish, and the last spike had been driven at mile 26.2 near Britannia Beach. Three trains filled with dignitaries, the press, and representatives from other railroad companies left North Vancouver to go to Porteau, just south of Britannia, for the driving of the copper spike on June 10, 1956. As well as the PGE cars there were cars from the Canadian National, Canadian Pacific, Great Northern, Northern Pacific, and Milwaukee railroads. The last sent a super dome car that fortunately passed through all the tunnels successfully. The first train was hauled by diesels 585 and 584, the second by diesels 581 and 582, and the third by 557. They left Porteau June 11 and went on to Squamish, returning the same day over the newly laid track. After forty-five years, the Burrard Inlet-Interior connection was finally complete.

Goodbye, PGE—Hello, BCR

It was April 1, 1972, when, in the words of BCR authority H.A. Armstrong, "the operations of the PGE passed into the pages of history with the introduction of a new name, the British Columbia Railway." The name was changed by Premier W.A.C. Bennett, who thought PGE did not denote "British Columbia" when the PGE cars traveled on tracks across the country. He felt "British Columbia" must be in the name of the railroad for public relations reasons.

Since 1972, the BCR has built two additional rail lines north: the Deas Lake Extension, 420 miles west of Fort St. James, and the 250-mile-long Fort Nelson Extension, which have now opened up areas of the province otherwise neglected by modern transportation. Further growth has resulted from the two national railways, the CN and CP, and the two major United States carriers, forming a close network linking the railway with the major points on this continent. This is invaluable, as seventy-nine percent of the railroad's freight revenue comes from the forest products that are shipped throughout North America.

The BCR now employs almost three thousand persons and has seven industrial parks. The parks serve industry at Williams Lake, Prince George, Fort St. James, Dawson Creek, Mackenzie, Fort St. John, and Fort Nelson. These, along with the car shop at Squamish, have brought employment to areas that needed a boost to their economy.

The growth along with the proposed coal developments in British Columbia's northeast region and the sulfur production at Taylor and Fort Nelson, account for a statement made by the company's President and Chief Executive Officer, Mackenzie Norris, who said, "The saga of the PGE-BCR has proven that the dreams of a provincial railroad to open up British Columbia's interior were not only justified, but very successful."

Now the British Columbia Railway has been joined by the Royal Hudson in bringing the beauties of the North Shore and Howe Sound to tourists and railroad buffs.

The Royal Hudson

The Royal Hudson has a riches-to-rags and a rags-to-riches history; the regal lady of the British Columbia rails came out of retirement after having pulled the CPR's long transcontinental passenger trains across the continent for fifteen years.

Why is it called the "Royal Hudson"? In 1939 her predecessor, the Hudson 2850 pulled the royal train carrying His Majesty King George VI and Queen Elizabeth across Canada on their first visit after his coronation. Impressed with the train's performance, King George gave his permission to designate the Hudson engines Royal Hudsons. The 2860 was the first engine to be built

The Royal Hudson at Castlegar, B.C.

after this designation.

It was 1955 when the Royal Hudson 2860 came to Vancouver at the instigation of Major Mathews and Alderman Emory of the Vancouver City Council, who were seeking an old train to be used as a monument to the steam age. The Royal Hudson was found sitting in the scrapyard in Montreal waiting to be converted to scrap, after diesel took the place of steam engines. She was covered in the dust and grime of a trainyard with weeds growing up around her. At a cost of twelve thousand dollars to city council, she was "spared" and brought to Vancouver.

Engine 2860 arrived in Vancouver and was set up at CPR's Drake Street shops, where holes, bent metal, and missing pieces were filled with putty. With a good patch job and a coat of paint, the engine looked quite elegant.

Ten years later the CPR asked Vancouver City Council to pay for their historic engine, and the council said, "No." So the engine was to be repossessed. Many people felt she should be kept, and two clubs were formed to try to retain the monument; one by the mayor, who in effect asked that anyone wishing to make a donation contribute to a fund to be set up at city hall. Another was called the 2860 Club and sought donations for the preservation of the old engine. However, Joe Hussey bought the engine for twelve thousand dollars from the CPR and formed the Royal Hudson Steam Train Club. Train buffs and interested citizens wanted to see her with steam up, and, after some public pressure, the British Columbia government approached Hussey, who agreed to sell the engine to the Province for twenty-five thousand dollars. The 2860 had been stripped of her crowns and name-plates, and she was in a sorry state because of the lack of repairs, scaling paint, and falling putty.

Tourism B.C.
Photo No. 43867-1979

The Royal Hudson above Howe Sound.

Laurie Wallace, Department of the Provincial Secretary, became interested in the government's purchase and, along with the ten to eleven thousand dollars collected by the clubs, a Royal Hudson Restoration Fund was established. For four to five months, eager workers, retired railroad men, and railroad buffs restored and repaired the 2860. After five months, they could no longer wait to get the Royal Hudson running. And it was to the delight of her devoted fans that the grand old lady of the rails steamed up and down the yard tracks.

The federal government also took an interest in the project and supplied some money. New tubes were purchased for the boiler, and Vancouver shipyards prepared the tubes to fit. When the day of the boiler inspection test came, the 2860 passed and was pronounced fit to run. The many months of hard work had paid off, to the gratification of the workers.

The next challenge was to find some coaches to accompany the Royal Hudson and make her a tourist attraction for those who were interested in traveling on a steam train. Fifteen old coaches, a tender, and a baggage car were found in the Glen Yards in Montreal and were purchased in a deal with the CPR for $120,000 f.o.b. Vancouver. They were hauled to Vancouver CPR yards and sat there waiting for repairs and refurbishing.

The Royal Hudson and coaches created a great deal of interest among railroad people. One devoted admirer, Bob Swanson, worked hard to bring to fruition the purchase of the Royal Hudson and coaches. In 1973, Swanson, a railroad buff and engineer, was able to persuade some CPR coach workers to work on the Royal Hudson on their own time. The expertise and knowledge of these men guaranteed a professional job and saved many dollars in the long run.

In about three months, six coaches were ready and the Royal Hudson Steam Train was ready for painting. It was decided to use the old CPR colors of black and dark red. The paint had had to be specially made up at the CPR's Montreal department.

The train looked very regal in shiny black, with red and gold trim and new emblems. British Columbia's coat of arms adorned the tender, while the engine carried a new smaller crest designed especially for the Royal Hudson by devotee Bob Swanson.

The Royal Hudson above Horseshoe Bay.

Steam rushes from the engine of the Royal Hudson as it makes its way back to Vancouver from Squamish, B.C.

June 20, 1974, was the day of the first trip for the Royal Hudson Steam Train to Squamish. Among the passengers were many VIPs, including B.C.'s Premier Dave Barrett. With much ceremony, the Royal Hudson moved out of the station in North Vancouver, gathered speed, and, pulling her fifteen coaches, chugged from North Vancouver on to Squamish.

Each of the coaches in the train was given a special name after places along the PGE-BCR tracks. The two private cars filled with the VIPs were once again the showplaces they had been. The Discovery car, named for the British ship *Discovery*, is a period coach with antique furnishings and fittings. The Brittania car, named for the old mining town on Howe Sound, is in modern decor and most suitable for business meetings. These cars can be booked for private parties.

The observation car is a gem. It is open at each end with the center one-third closed.

The Royal Hudson Steam Train now boasts the 2860 and tender, the box car Prince George, and fifteen coaches. All coaches are in excellent condition and the decor pleasing. Upholstered seats, old-time pictures, and the old engine sounds give the passengers a feeling of going back in time.

The fact that the Royal Hudson Steam Train is a great tourist attraction is attested to by the long waiting list for reservations. The train carries about sixty-eight passengers per car, for a total of 950 people in the entire train. In a year approximately sixty thousand passengers enjoy the train as it travels along the track to Squamish. The price per ticket has remained at eight dollars return.

The idea of the Royal Hudson was to create a tourist attraction that offered spectacular scenery, comfort, a two-hour stop at Squamish, and return for a modest fee. In this it succeeds, exceeding the highest expectations of all who have labored to make the Royal Hudson 2860 the queen of the tracks.